Explorations In
Careers
Without
College

By Brandy Champeau and Nancy Holt
Illustrated by Hatice Bayramoglu
Exploring Expression

ISBN-13: 978-1-954057-15-9

Table of Contents

Introduction

CAREERS WITHOUT COLLEGE: INTRODUCTION

Welcome to Explorations in Careers Without College!

Remember when you were younger, and the grown-ups would ask you what you wanted to be when you grew up? At that time, you answered from your limited knowledge of the world and career choices. Doctor, policeman, teacher, race car driver, pro baseball player . . . . .

But now you are getting closer to the time when you should be thinking seriously about the choices available to you. For many people the automatic response involves questions like "where will you go to college" or "What will you study"? However, there are many valuable, viable careers that require no college at all. College is not a prerequisite for success.

One limitation in your search for college-free career possibilities is that there are so many jobs out there that you may not realize don't require a college degree to enter the field. This is where this book comes it. The intent of this book is to introduce you to some of the familiar and less familiar professions that can lead to fulfilling careers without any college degree at all.

This book is created with the intent that YOU do the research. To simply name a career field and tell you its definition does little for you as you examine possibilities. By doing some research on your own, forcing yourself to look past just answering the simple questions, you will see more than just surface knowledge. Perhaps something will catch your eye that excites your imagination.

Suggestions for Using This Book:

Stand-Alone Elective Course: This book examines 37 career fields. By researching at least one per week, a student will complete sufficient hours of work to qualify for an elective requirement. By including videos and field trips to see people working in these jobs, the student should have a well-rounded knowledge of potential fields open to them.

Supplemental Course Material: This book can also be used to supplement another curriculum a student may be taking. Students and/or instructors can choose to research careers to pertain to the material they are studying in other studies. *This course makes a perfect accompaniment to the Country Plus Core Curriculum by Exploring Expression*

Guided Journal/Workbook: This book can be used outside of a classroom environment by someone interested in exploring career possibilities. Whether you are looking for your own future or wanting to be able to provide guidance and counseling for others' explorations, this book takes you past the common groups of jobs, helping you to learn about possibilities often overlooked.

Contents of Each Career Section

Informational Pages

- **Career short description.**
- **Career Spotlight. This is a starting point for your career research.** We have provided a selection of websites and videos to help get you started in your exploration of each career. These resources will give you a great overview of the career. However, these are intended to be a starting point on your exploration. We encourage you to branch out with other websites and videos as well as interviews and field trips as applicable to give yourself a fuller immersion into each career.

Assignment Pages

Part 1: General Information

The first step in your examination of a career field is to gather some basic information about it.

- **What is the career?** Define it in your own words after viewing the online material.

- **Job Duties and Specialization: What are some of the specialty areas in this field?** It is one thing to say that someone is a doctor, but that is too vague. The medical profession has so many specialties that should be considered as options. People who feint at the sight of blood may not make great surgeons, but they could become highly successful psychiatrists. Lawyers can specialize in criminal, contract, corporate, and even tax law. Every field has specialties that, if known, could change your whole outlook on the field.

- **Work Environment: What is the Work Environment?** Is it indoor work or outdoors? Is it primarily a sedentary job (sitting at a desk) or one that requires physical movement or manual labor? Do you have to be in a specific region of the world or climate to do the work? Would you work alone or be involved with other groups or the general public?

- **Income Potential:** How much money can you expect to make in this career field. What is the income growth potential between starting out and experienced?

Part 2: Detailed Information

In Part 2 research, you will dig a little deeper into the nuances of the field.

- **Educational Requirements:** Is this a field that requires a 4 year or graduate degree? Is this a skills-based career that is taught in a vocational school, or does it require some artistic talent? Perhaps it's a field that requires years of on-the-job training to become an apprentice, journeyman, or master craftsman. Unless you are a phenomenon like Kobe Bryant, many professional athletes must succeed on college teams before being drafted to pros.

- **Special Skills:** Are there skills or talents that enhance one's probability for success? Do you need to be a good writer, be a whiz on computers, love animals, or be able to lift heavy objects? An engineer needs to be good at math; a singer will have difficulty if they are tone deaf. What phobias would make this a poor choice (such as a person with a fear of heights may not be happy repairing radio or cell phone towers).

- **Tools Used: What kind of tools are used in this career?** Are there any special items or software that are required or even helpful in performing the duties of this career?

- **Career Progression: What is the career progression?** Not everyone can afford to go to school for 10 years to become a PhD before starting their adult work life. Most of us progress in a field. What type of work would someone just entering a profession do? What does it take to move up in the field, and what are some of the mid-range and senior positions available for those with the time, training and experience?

- **Future Outlook: Is this an enduring field?** Changes in technology are changing the job market. And anyone looking toward the future should consider the "What if" scenarios. What is the outlook for this type of work in 10 or 20 years?

- **Other Facts:** This section lets you list any other interesting tidbits that you have discovered about this career. Perhaps there is a famous person or a relative in this career field. Maybe this career was in the news recently or had some leaps in technology or procedure. Any other interesting information you find goes here.

Part 3: Personal Assessment

This is where you personalize the information you have learned about the career. In Part 3, you will take the information gathered and evaluate it in terms of your own interests.

- **What are the positive aspects of this career?** Think about what you learned. Is there anything that sounds interesting? Is there anything that you think you'd excel at?

- **What are the negative aspects of this career?** What about this career sounds unbearable to you? What would be an obstacle for you if pursuing this line of work?

- **Is this a career worth your further consideration?** Go ahead - pass judgement. Does this career excite you or pique your interest? Be practical—while the sky is the limit for your future, do you see yourself as willing to take the time, energy and even money to succeed at this line of work? Obstacles and challenges can be overcome, but is this interesting enough to motivate you to do whatever is whatever is necessary to overcome those challenges?

Remember, what you decide about any career option is not set in stone. A definite NO today doesn't mean you won't learn something later that opens your mind to new possibilities. Saying all 36 of the careers in this book all have potential is just as valid as saying none of them do. It's not the decisions you make as much as the understanding you gain that allows you to grow through this course.

HAVE FUN WITH THIS RESEARCH—THINK, LEARN, EXPLORE, AND OPEN YOUR EYES TO ALL SORTS OF POSSIBILITIES.

Careers

POLICE OFFICER

POLICE

A police officer enforces the law by arresting criminals and detecting and preventing crimes.

POLICE OFFICER

Suggested Websites and Videos:

Police and Detectives:

https://wwwblsgov/ooh/protective-service/police-and-detectiveshtm

Private detectives and investigators:

https://wwwblsgov/ooh/protective-service/private-detectives-and-investigatorshtm

Correctional Officers and Bailiffs:

https://wwwblsgov/ooh/protective-service/correctional-officershtm

33-305101 - Police Patrol Officers:

https://wwwyoutubecom/watch?v=14D91NPvMz8&feature=emb_logo

Private Detectives and Investigators Career Video:

https://wwwyoutubecom/watch?v=PNOImo84oHI&feature=emb_logo

Correctional Officers, Jailers, and Bailiffs Video:

https://wwwyoutubecom/watch?v=Vcnk_bSJsAc&t=51s

PART 1:
GENERAL INFORMATION

In your own words, define this career.

_____

_____

_____

_____

Job Duties:

_____

_____

_____

_____

_____

_____

_____

Work Environment:

Tools Used:

PART 2:
DETAILED INFORMATION

Education Needed:

_____
_____
_____
_____
_____
_____
_____
_____
_____
_____
_____
_____
_____

Special Skills:

_____
_____
_____
_____
_____
_____
_____
_____
_____
_____
_____
_____

Career Progression:

PART 2:
DETAILED INFORMATION

Future Outlook:

Other Facts about this Career

_____
_____
_____
_____
_____
_____
_____
_____
_____

PART 3:
PERSONAL ASSESSMENT

Positive Aspects:

_____

_____

_____

_____

Negative Aspects:

_____

_____

_____

_____

Is this Career for you? Why/why not?

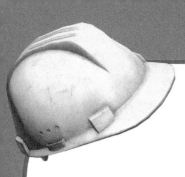

A <u>Firefighter</u> controls and puts out fires and responds to emergencies.

Suggested Websites and Videos:

BLS firefighter:

> https://wwwblsgov/ooh/protective-service/firefightershtm

Onetonline firefighters:

> https://wwwonetonlineorg/link/summary/33-201100

BIA Fire & Forestry

> https://wwwbiagov/bia/ots/dfwfm/bwfm/job-information

Firefighters Career Video:

> https://wwwyoutubecom/watch?v=DNK5dYGn3Fg

Firefighter - Career Video:

> https://www.youtube.com/watch?v=XeLwoyVIqUE

BIA Fire and Aviation Recruitment Video:

> https://wwwyoutubecom/watch?v=c8VnzD87Qj8

PART 1:
GENERAL INFORMATION

In your own words, define this career.

_____
_____
_____
_____

Job Duties:

_____
_____
_____
_____
_____
_____
_____

Work Environment:

Tools Used:

PART 2:
DETAILED INFORMATION

Education Needed:

_____
_____
_____
_____
_____
_____
_____
_____
_____
_____
_____

Special Skills:

_____
_____
_____
_____
_____
_____
_____
_____
_____
_____
_____
_____

Career Progression:

PART 2:
DETAILED INFORMATION

Future Outlook:

Other Facts about this Career

_____
_____
_____
_____
_____
_____
_____
_____
_____
_____

PART 3:
PERSONAL ASSESSMENT

Positive Aspects:

_____
_____
_____
_____

Negative Aspects:

_____
_____
_____
_____

Is this Career for you? Why/why not?

An EMT (Emergency Medical Technician) responds to calls for emergency medical assistance.

Suggested Websites and Videos:

EMTs and Paramedics
    https://wwwblsgov/ooh/healthcare/emts-and-paramedicshtm
Emergency Medical Technicians:
    https://wwwonetonlineorg/link/summary/29-204200
EMS Careers:
    https://wwwnaemtorg/about-ems/careers
Emergency Medical Technicians and Paramedics Career Video:
    https://wwwyoutubecom/watch?v=C8zIHk9KKqI
What is a EMT? What is a Paramedic? (What do EMTs Do, How To
Become a Paramedic, EMTs Career Advice):
    https://wwwyoutubecom/watch?v=pfbJSyPI6tM
EMS Career Plan | EMT Jobs | Paramedic Jobs | EMT/Paramedic:
    https://wwwyoutubecom/watch?v=va7h1aTy6nE

PART 1:
GENERAL INFORMATION

In your own words, define this career.

_____

_____

_____

_____

Job Duties:

_____

_____

_____

_____

_____

_____

_____

Work Environment:

Tools Used:

PART 2:
DETAILED INFORMATION

Education Needed:

_____
_____
_____
_____
_____
_____
_____
_____
_____
_____
_____
_____

Special Skills:

_____
_____
_____
_____
_____
_____
_____
_____
_____
_____
_____
_____
_____

Career Progression:

PART 2:
DETAILED INFORMATION

Future Outlook:

Other Facts about this Career

_____
_____
_____
_____
_____
_____
_____
_____
_____

PART 3:
PERSONAL ASSESSMENT

Positive Aspects:

_____

_____

_____

_____

Negative Aspects:

_____

_____

_____

_____

Is this Career for you? Why/why not?

SOLDIER

A <u>Soldier</u> is a member of the military who protects his or her country during war and peacetime.

SOLDIER

Suggested Websites and Videos:

Military Careers:

https://www.bls.gov/ooh/military/military-careers.htm#tab-2

Advanced Individual Training:

https://www.goarmy.com/careers-and-jobs/job-training/advanced-individual-training.html

General Requirements:

https://www.marines.com/become-a-marine/requirements/general.html

Requirements:

https://www.marines.com/become-a-marine/requirements/general.html

Military - Career Video:

https://www.youtube.com/watch?v=s0-HzvLDe6o

PART 1:
GENERAL INFORMATION

In your own words, define this career.

_____
_____
_____
_____

Job Duties:

_____
_____
_____
_____
_____
_____
_____

Work Environment:

Tools Used:

PART 2:
DETAILED INFORMATION

Education Needed:

_____
_____
_____
_____
_____
_____
_____
_____
_____
_____
_____
_____

Special Skills:

_____
_____
_____
_____
_____
_____
_____
_____
_____
_____
_____
_____

Career Progression:

PART 2:
DETAILED INFORMATION

Future Outlook:

Other Facts about this Career

PART 3:
PERSONAL ASSESSMENT

Positive Aspects:

_____

_____

_____

_____

Negative Aspects:

_____

_____

_____

_____

Is this Career for you? Why/why not?

A Licensed Practical Nurse (LPN) provides patients with primary and essential care, including monitoring vital signs.

Suggested Websites and Videos:

Nurses:

https://www.bls.gov/ooh/healthcare/licensed-practical-and-licensed-vocational-nurses.htm

Licensed Practical and Licensed Vocational Nurses

https://www.onetonline.org/link/summary/29-2061.00

Requirements, Duties, And Perks: An In-depth Exploration Of The LPN Role

https://nightingale.edu/blog/lpn-nurse/

Licensed Practical and Licensed Vocational Nurses Career Video:

https://www.youtube.com/watch?v=yTBPYOnNjVU&t=2s

Licensed Practical Nurse (LPN), Career Video from drkit.org:

https://www.youtube.com/watch?v=-Jszunbitog

Licensed Practical Nurse (Episode 101)

https://www.youtube.com/watch?v=fUdiEP-FD9g

PART 1:
GENERAL INFORMATION

In your own words, define this career.

_____
_____
_____
_____

Job Duties:

_____
_____
_____
_____
_____
_____
_____

Work Environment:

Tools Used:

PART 2:
DETAILED INFORMATION

Education Needed:

_____
_____
_____
_____
_____
_____
_____
_____
_____
_____
_____

Special Skills:

_____
_____
_____
_____
_____
_____
_____
_____
_____
_____

Career Progression:

PART 2:
DETAILED INFORMATION

Future Outlook:

Other Facts about this Career

_____
_____
_____
_____
_____
_____
_____
_____
_____
_____

PART 3:
PERSONAL ASSESSMENT

Positive Aspects:

_____

_____

_____

_____

Negative Aspects:

_____

_____

_____

_____

Is this Career for you? Why/why not?

A Dental Hygienist

examines patients for signs of oral diseases and provides preventive care.

Suggested Websites and Videos:

Dental Hygienists:
https://www.bls.gov/ooh/healthcare/dental-hygienists.htm

29-1292.00 - Dental Hygienists
https://www.onetonline.org/link/summary/29-1292.00

Dental Hygienists:
https://www.careeronestop.org/Toolkit/Careers/Occupations/occupation-
profile.aspx?keyword=Dental%20Hygienists&onetcode=29129200
&location=UNITED%20STATES

Dental Hygienists Career Video
https://www.youtube.com/watch?v=TeAtDfCQ0J4

Dental Hygienist - Video:
https://www.youtube.com/watch?v=kt4_B3btZCc

Dental Hygienist, Career Video from drkit.org
https://www.youtube.com/watch?v=QKPqfF4vKos

PART 1:
GENERAL INFORMATION

In your own words, define this career.

_____

_____

_____

_____

Job Duties:

_____

_____

_____

_____

_____

_____

_____

_____

Work Environment:

Tools Used:

PART 2:
DETAILED INFORMATION

Education Needed:

_____
_____
_____
_____
_____
_____
_____
_____
_____
_____

Special Skills:

_____
_____
_____
_____
_____
_____
_____
_____
_____
_____
_____

Career Progression:

PART 2:
DETAILED INFORMATION

Future Outlook:

Other Facts about this Career

_____
_____
_____
_____
_____
_____
_____
_____
_____
_____

PART 3:
PERSONAL ASSESSMENT

Positive Aspects:

_____

_____

_____

_____

Negative Aspects:

_____

_____

_____

_____

Is this Career for you? Why/why not?

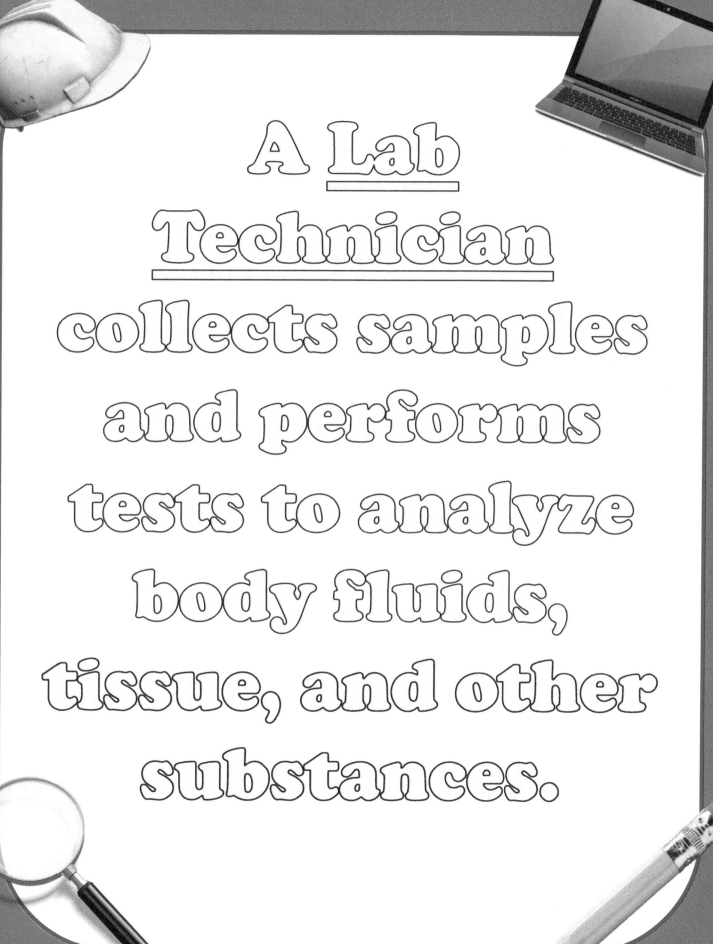

A <u>Lab Technician</u> collects samples and performs tests to analyze body fluids, tissue, and other substances.

LAB TECHNICIAN

Suggested Websites and Videos:

Clinical Laboratory Technologists and Technicians:
https://www.bls.gov/ooh/healthcare/clinical-laboratory-technologists-and-technicians.htm

Medical and Clinical Laboratory Technicians
https://www.onetonline.org/link/summary/29-2012.00

Career Profile: Medical Laboratory Technician:
https://www.cambridgehealth.edu/career-profile-medical-laboratory-technician/

Dental Hygienists:
https://www.careeronestop.org/Toolkit/Careers/Occupations/occupation-profile.aspx?keyword=Dental%20Hygienists&location=UNITED%20STATES&onetcode=29129200

Medical and Clinical Laboratory Technologists Career Video
https://www.youtube.com/watch?v=tm2KBoKns78&t=2s

Medical Laboratory Technician, Career Video from drkit.org:
https://www.youtube.com/watch?v=I6O189p1Tjg

Dental and Ophthalmic Laboratory Technician Career Video
https://www.youtube.com/watch?v=9El6cags1O4

PART 1:
GENERAL INFORMATION

In your own words, define this career.

_____
_____
_____
_____

Job Duties:

_____
_____
_____
_____
_____
_____
_____
_____

Work Environment:

Tools Used:

PART 2:
DETAILED INFORMATION

Education Needed:

_____
_____
_____
_____
_____
_____
_____
_____
_____
_____
_____
_____
_____

Special Skills:

_____
_____
_____
_____
_____
_____
_____
_____
_____
_____
_____
_____
_____

Career Progression:

PART 2:
DETAILED INFORMATION

Future Outlook:

Other Facts about this Career

_____
_____
_____
_____
_____
_____
_____
_____
_____
_____

PART 3: PERSONAL ASSESSMENT

Positive Aspects:

_____
_____
_____
_____

Negative Aspects:

_____
_____
_____
_____

Is this Career for you? Why/why not?

CARPENTER

A Carpenter

constructs, repairs, and installs furniture, building frameworks and structures made from wood and other materials.

CARPENTER

Suggested Websites and Videos:

Carpenters:
https://www.bls.gov/ooh/construction-and-extraction/carpenters.htm

Carpenters:
https://www.careeronestop.org/Toolkit/Careers/Occupations/occupation-profile.aspx?keyword=Carpenters&location=KENTUCKY&onetcode=47203100

Carpenters:
https://www.onetonline.org/link/summary/47-2031.00

Carpenters Career Video:
https://www.youtube.com/watch?v=i-tiC2Y-038

Carpenter Career Video:
https://www.youtube.com/watch?v=-_kZ1HY4J6I

Cabinetmakers and Bench Carpenters (Woodworkers) Career Video:
https://www.youtube.com/watch?v=Avn11IVTieY

PART 1:
GENERAL INFORMATION

In your own words, define this career.

_____
_____
_____
_____

Job Duties:

_____
_____
_____
_____
_____
_____
_____

Work Environment:

Tools Used:

PART 2:
DETAILED INFORMATION

Education Needed:

_____
_____
_____
_____
_____
_____
_____
_____
_____
_____

Special Skills:

_____
_____
_____
_____
_____
_____
_____
_____
_____
_____
_____
_____

Career Progression:

Part 2:
Detailed Information

Future Outlook:

Other Facts about this Career

PART 3:
PERSONAL ASSESSMENT

Positive Aspects:

_____
_____
_____
_____

Negative Aspects:

_____
_____
_____
_____

Is this Career for you? Why/why not?

A <u>Plumber</u>

installs and repairs water, gas, and other piping systems in homes, businesses, and factories.

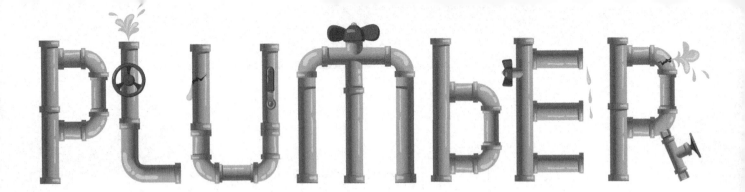

PLUMBER

Suggested Websites and Videos:

Plumbers, Pipefitters, and Steamfitters:
https://www.careeronestop.org/Toolkit/Careers/Occupations/occupation-profile.aspx?keyword=Plumbers,%20Pipefitters,%20and%20Steamfitters&onetcode=47215200&location=UNITED%20STATES

Plumbers, Pipefitters, and Steamfitters:
https://www.bls.gov/ooh/construction-and-extraction/plumbers-pipefitters-and-steamfitters.htm

Plumbers, Pipefitters, and Steamfitters:
https://www.onetonline.org/link/summary/47-2152.00

Plumbers, Pipefitters, and Steamfitters Career Video:
https://www.youtube.com/watch?v=uF3-2wFnf0E

What do Plumbers Do? A Plumbing Trade Career with the UA:
https://www.youtube.com/watch?v=fgAnrLxMTsc

Plumber, Career Video from drkit.org:
https://www.youtube.com/watch?v=bDegV91AawYm

PART 1:
GENERAL INFORMATION

In your own words, define this career.

_____

_____

_____

_____

Job Duties:

_____

_____

_____

_____

_____

_____

_____

Work Environment:

Tools Used:

PART 2:
DETAILED INFORMATION

Education Needed:

_____
_____
_____
_____
_____
_____
_____
_____
_____
_____
_____
_____

Special Skills:

_____
_____
_____
_____
_____
_____
_____
_____
_____
_____
_____
_____
_____
_____

Career Progression:

PART 2:
DETAILED INFORMATION

Future Outlook:

Other Facts about this Career

PART 3:
PERSONAL ASSESSMENT

Positive Aspects:

_____
_____
_____
_____

Negative Aspects:

_____
_____
_____
_____

Is this Career for you? Why/why not?

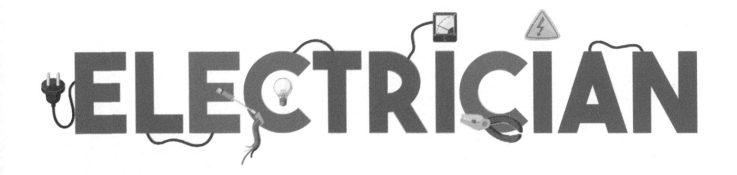

ELECTRICIAN

An Electrician

installs, maintains, and repairs electrical power, communications, lighting, and control systems.

ELECTRICIAN

Suggested Websites and Videos:

Electricians:
https://www.bls.gov/ooh/construction-and-extraction/electricians.htm

Electricians:
https://www.careeronestop.org/Toolkit/Careers/Occupations/occupation-profile.aspx?keyword=Electricians&location=UNITED%20STATES&lang=en&onetcode=47211100

Electricians:
https://www.onetonline.org/link/summary/47-2111.00

Electricians Career Video:
https://www.youtube.com/watch?v=Rw8gAGYZ6qs

Electrician Career Video:
https://www.youtube.com/watch?v=9Luo1qJNFUY

Electrician, Career Video from drkit.org:
https://www.youtube.com/watch?v=skEyasonpiM

Part 1:
General Information

In your own words, define this career.

_____
_____
_____
_____

Job Duties:

_____
_____
_____
_____
_____
_____
_____

Work Environment:

Tools Used:

PART 2:
DETAILED INFORMATION

Education Needed:

_____
_____
_____
_____
_____
_____
_____
_____
_____
_____
_____
_____

Special Skills:

_____
_____
_____
_____
_____
_____
_____
_____
_____
_____
_____

Career Progression:

PART 2:
DETAILED INFORMATION

Future Outlook:

Other Facts about this Career

_____
_____
_____
_____
_____
_____
_____
_____
_____

PART 3:
PERSONAL ASSESSMENT

Positive Aspects:

_____
_____
_____
_____

Negative Aspects:

_____
_____
_____
_____

Is this Career for you? Why/why not?

A <u>Mason</u> uses bricks, concrete and concrete blocks, and natural and manmade stones to build walkways, walls, and other structures.

Suggested Websites and Videos:

Brick Masons and Block Masons:
> https://www.careeronestop.org/Toolkit/Careers/Occupations/occupation-profile.aspx?keyword=Brickmasons%20and%20Blockmasons&onetcode=47202100&location=UNITED%20STATES

Masonry Workers:
> https://www.bls.gov/ooh/construction-and-extraction/brickmasons-blockmasons-and-stonemasons.htm

Cement Masons and Concrete Finishers:
> https://www.onetonline.org/link/summary/47-2051.00

Brick Masons and Block Masons Career Video:
> https://www.youtube.com/watch?v=Un7U4gej3j0

Plasterer and Stucco Mason Career Video:
> https://www.youtube.com/watch?v=PkIYLvoSRNQ

Plasterer and Stucco Mason Career Video IYI(India Youth Institute):
> https://www.youtube.com/watch?v=D-3EmYeF0jM

PART 1:
GENERAL INFORMATION

In your own words, define this career.

_____
_____
_____
_____

Job Duties:

_____
_____
_____
_____
_____
_____
_____
_____

Work Environment:

Tools Used:

PART 2:
DETAILED INFORMATION

Education Needed:

_____
_____
_____
_____
_____
_____
_____
_____
_____
_____
_____
_____

Special Skills:

_____
_____
_____
_____
_____
_____
_____
_____
_____
_____
_____

Career Progression:

PART 2:
DETAILED INFORMATION

Future Outlook:

Other Facts about this Career

_____

_____

_____

_____

_____

_____

_____

_____

_____

PART 3:
PERSONAL ASSESSMENT

Positive Aspects:

_____
_____
_____
_____

Negative Aspects:

_____
_____
_____
_____

Is this Career for you? Why/why not?

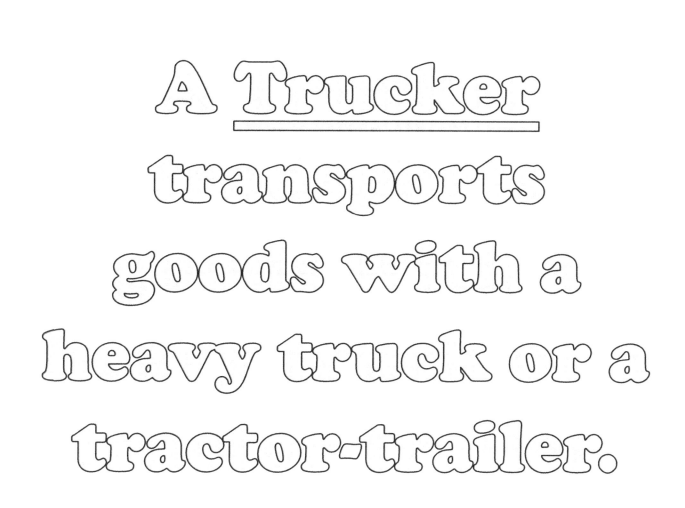

A <u>Trucker</u> transports goods with a heavy truck or a tractor-trailer.

TRUCKER

Suggested Websites and Videos:

Heavy and Tractor-Trailer Truck Drivers:
https://www.careeronestop.org/toolkit/careers/occupations/occupation-profile.aspx?keyword=Heavy%20and%20Tractor-Trailer%20Truck%20Drivers&onetcode=53303200&location=UNITED%20STATES

Light Truck Drivers:
https://www.careeronestop.org/Toolkit/Careers/Occupations/occupation-profile.aspx?keyword=Light%20Truck%20Drivers&onetcode=53303300&location=US

Driver/Sales Workers:
https://www.onetonline.org/link/summary/53-3031.00

Truck Drivers - Heavy and Tractor-Trailer Career Video:
https://www.youtube.com/watch?v=yz8Oku9fQfQ

Driver/Sales Workers:
https://www.youtube.com/watch?v=wHn2S2wzYjk

Light Truck and Delivery Driver/Sales Workers Career Video:
https://www.youtube.com/watch?v=nhDMoNCrniA

Delivery Truck Drivers and Driver/Sales Workers:
https://www.bls.gov/ooh/transportation-and-material-moving/delivery-truck-drivers-and-driver-sales-workers.htm

PART 1:
GENERAL INFORMATION

In your own words, define this career.

_____
_____
_____
_____

Job Duties:

_____
_____
_____
_____
_____
_____
_____
_____

Work Environment:

Tools Used:

PART 2:
DETAILED INFORMATION

Education Needed:

_____
_____
_____
_____
_____
_____
_____
_____
_____
_____
_____

Special Skills:

_____
_____
_____
_____
_____
_____
_____
_____
_____
_____
_____
_____

Career Progression:

PART 2:
DETAILED INFORMATION

Future Outlook:

Other Facts about this Career

_____
_____
_____
_____
_____
_____
_____
_____
_____
_____

PART 3:
PERSONAL ASSESSMENT

Positive Aspects:

_____

_____

_____

_____

Negative Aspects:

_____

_____

_____

_____

Is this Career for you? Why/why not?

A <u>Mechanic</u>

inspects, maintains, and repairs cars and trucks.

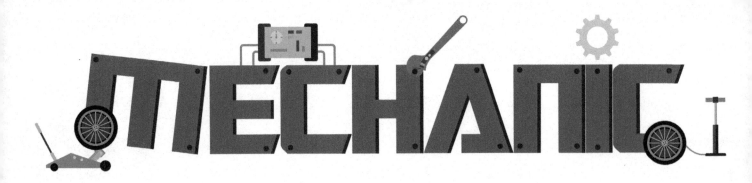

Suggested Websites and Videos:

Heavy and Tractor-Trailer Truck Drivers:
https://www.careeronestop.org/toolkit/careers/occupations/occupation-profile.aspx?keyword=Heavy%20and%20Tractor-Trailer%20Truck%20Drivers&onetcode=53303200&location=UNITED%20STATES

Light Truck Drivers:
https://www.careeronestop.org/Toolkit/Careers/Occupations/occupation-profile.aspx?keyword=Light%20Truck%20Drivers&onetcode=53303300&location=US

Driver/Sales Workers:
https://www.onetonline.org/link/summary/53-3031.00

Truck Drivers - Heavy and Tractor-Trailer Career Video:
https://www.youtube.com/watch?v=yz8Oku9fQfQ

Driver/Sales Workers:
https://www.youtube.com/watch?v=wHn2S2wzYjk

Light Truck and Delivery Driver/Sales Workers Career Video:
https://www.youtube.com/watch?v=nhDMoNCrniA

Delivery Truck Drivers and Driver/Sales Workers:
https://www.bls.gov/ooh/transportation-and-material-moving/delivery-truck-drivers-and-driver-sales-workers.htm

PART 1:
GENERAL INFORMATION

In your own words, define this career.

_____
_____
_____
_____

Job Duties:

_____
_____
_____
_____
_____
_____
_____
_____

Work Environment:

Tools Used:

PART 2:
DETAILED INFORMATION

Education Needed:

_____
_____
_____
_____
_____
_____
_____
_____
_____
_____
_____
_____

Special Skills:

_____
_____
_____
_____
_____
_____
_____
_____
_____
_____
_____

Career Progression:

PART 2:
DETAILED INFORMATION

Future Outlook:

Other Facts about this Career

_____
_____
_____
_____
_____
_____
_____
_____
_____
_____

PART 3:
PERSONAL ASSESSMENT

Positive Aspects:

_____

_____

_____

_____

Negative Aspects:

_____

_____

_____

_____

Is this Career for you? Why/why not?

A **Flight Attendant** is in charge of the cabin in an aircraft, and is responsible for the safety and comfort of the passengers.

Suggested Websites and Videos:

Flight Attendants:
https://www.bls.gov/ooh/transportation-and-material-moving/flight-attendants.htm

Flight Attendants COS (CareerOneStop):
https://www.careeronestop.org/Toolkit/Careers/Occupations/occupation-profile.aspx?keyword=Flight%20Attendants&location=UNITED%20STATES&onetcode=53203100

Flight Attendants One:
https://www.onetonline.org/link/summary/53-2031.00

Flight Attendants Career Video:
https://www.youtube.com/watch?v=S6a3XVIMnHE

Flight Attendant, Career Video from drkit.org
https://www.youtube.com/watch?v=al5P_UHWvG4

Flight Attendant Career Video:
https://www.youtube.com/watch?v=EHbXkaJxGY0

PART 1:
GENERAL INFORMATION

In your own words, define this career.

_____
_____
_____
_____

Job Duties:

_____
_____
_____
_____
_____
_____
_____
_____

Work Environment:

Tools Used:

PART 2:
DETAILED INFORMATION

Education Needed:

_____
_____
_____
_____
_____
_____
_____
_____
_____
_____
_____
_____

Special Skills:

_____
_____
_____
_____
_____
_____
_____
_____
_____
_____

Career Progression:

PART 2:
DETAILED INFORMATION

Future Outlook:

Other Facts about this Career

_____

_____

_____

_____

_____

_____

_____

_____

_____

Part 3:
Personal Assessment

Positive Aspects:

_____
_____
_____
_____

Negative Aspects:

_____
_____
_____
_____

Is this Career for you? Why/why not?

PILOT

A **Pilot** flies and navigates airplanes, helicopters, and other types of aircraft.

Suggested Websites and Videos:

Airline and Commercial Pilots:

https://www.bls.gov/ooh/transportation-and-material-moving/airline-and-commercial-pilots.htm#tab-1

Commercial Pilots:

https://www.onetonline.org/link/summary/53-2012.00

Airline Pilots, Copilots, and Flight Engineers:

https://www.onetonline.org/link/summary/53-2011.00

United – Captain your career as a United pilot:

https://www.youtube.com/watch?v=sKXBZ2OW26M

Airline and Commercial Pilots:

https://www.youtube.com/watch?v=oey4mi_QV48

Commercial Pilot, Career Video from drkit.org:

https://www.youtube.com/watch?v=TXeICIY-qvY

Part 1:
General Information

In your own words, define this career.

_____
_____
_____
_____

Job Duties:

_____
_____
_____
_____
_____
_____
_____
_____

Work Environment:

Tools Used:

PART 2:
DETAILED INFORMATION

Education Needed:

_____
_____
_____
_____
_____
_____
_____
_____
_____
_____
_____

Special Skills:

_____
_____
_____
_____
_____
_____
_____
_____
_____
_____
_____

Career Progression:

PART 2:
DETAILED INFORMATION

Future Outlook:

Other Facts about this Career

_____

_____

_____

_____

_____

_____

_____

_____

_____

_____

PART 3:
PERSONAL ASSESSMENT

Positive Aspects:

_____
_____
_____
_____

Negative Aspects:

_____
_____
_____
_____

Is this Career for you? Why/why not?

SAILOR

A <u>Sailor</u> is someone who works on passenger ships, freighters, tanker ships and navy ships.

SAILOR

Suggested Websites and Videos:

Water Transportation Workers:
https://www.bls.gov/ooh/transportation-and-material-moving/water-transportation-occupations.htm

Sailors and Marine Oilers:
https://www.careeronestop.org/Toolkit/Careers/Occupations/occupation-profile.aspx?keyword=Sailors%20and%20Marine%20Oilers&location=WI&onetcode=53501100

Sailors and Marine Oilers:
https://www.onetonline.org/link/summary/53-5011.00

Sailors, Marine Oilers, and Ship Engineers Career Video:
https://www.youtube.com/watch?v=GaAw1VPGQfg

Sailors Careers Overview:
https://www.youtube.com/watch?v=d3gDmAmc7-o

Captains, Mates and Pilots of Water Vessels Career Video:
https://www.youtube.com/watch?v=V2zvpJucsK4

PART 1:
GENERAL INFORMATION

In your own words, define this career.

_____
_____
_____
_____

Job Duties:

_____
_____
_____
_____
_____
_____
_____

Work Environment:

Tools Used:

PART 2:
DETAILED INFORMATION

Education Needed:

_____
_____
_____
_____
_____
_____
_____
_____
_____
_____
_____

Special Skills:

_____
_____
_____
_____
_____
_____
_____
_____
_____
_____
_____

Career Progression:

PART 2:
DETAILED INFORMATION

Future Outlook:

Other Facts about this Career

_____
_____
_____
_____
_____
_____
_____
_____
_____
_____

PART 3:
PERSONAL ASSESSMENT

Positive Aspects:

_____

_____

_____

_____

Negative Aspects:

_____

_____

_____

_____

Is this Career for you? Why/why not?

MAILMAN

A <u>Mailman</u> collects and delivers letters, packages, and products to residences and businesses.

Suggested Websites and Videos:

Postal Service Workers:

https://www.bls.gov/ooh/office-and-administrative-support/postal-service-workers.htm#:~:text=The%20median%20annual%20wage%20for,was%20%2451%2C150%20in%20May%202020.&text=Overall%20employment%20of%20postal%20service,on%20average%2C%20over%20the%20decade

Postmasters and Mail Superintendents:

https://www.careeronestop.org/Toolkit/Careers/Occupations/occupation-profile.aspx?keyword=Postmasters%20and%20Mail%20Superintendents&onetcode=11913100&location=Utah

Postal Service Mail Carriers

https://www.careeronestop.org/toolkit/careers/occupations/occupation-profile.aspx?keyword=Postal%20Service%20Mail%20Carriers&onetcode=43505200&location=US

Postal Service Mail Sorter Career Video:

https://www.youtube.com/watch?v=xbPbKvQiOx0

Mailman Career Video:

https://www.youtube.com/watch?v=P9q3m-JNA64

Mail and Postal Service Career Video:

https://www.youtube.com/watch?v=ddvVveMJ2mw

PART 1:
GENERAL INFORMATION

In your own words, define this career.

_____

_____

_____

_____

Job Duties:

_____

_____

_____

_____

_____

_____

_____

Work Environment:

Tools Used:

PART 2:
DETAILED INFORMATION

Education Needed:

_____
_____
_____
_____
_____
_____
_____
_____
_____
_____
_____
_____

Special Skills:

_____
_____
_____
_____
_____
_____
_____
_____
_____
_____
_____

Career Progression:

PART 2:
DETAILED INFORMATION

Future Outlook:

Other Facts about this Career

_____
_____
_____
_____
_____
_____
_____
_____
_____
_____

PART 3:
PERSONAL ASSESSMENT

Positive Aspects:

_____

_____

_____

_____

Negative Aspects:

_____

_____

_____

_____

Is this Career for you? Why/why not?

A Train Engineer is responsible for driving passenger and freight trains safely from one destination to another.

Suggested Websites and Videos:

Rail Yard Engineers, Dinkey Operators, and Hostlers:
https://www.onetonline.org/link/summary/53-4013.00

Locomotive Engineers:
https://www.careeronestop.org/toolkit/careers/occupations/Occupation-
profile.aspx?keyword=Locomotive%20Engineers&onetcode=53401100&location=Washington&onet=53401100

Railroad Workers:
https://www.bls.gov/ooh/transportation-and-material-moving/railroad-occupations.htm

Locomotive Engineer : A unique career:
https://www.youtube.com/watch?v=QIbcdFQjSNo

Locomotive Engineers, Railroad Conductors and Yardmasters Career Video:
https://www.youtube.com/watch?v=oQBg-MVjxkU

HOW DO I GET A RAILROAD JOB? Conductor or Engineer? 2019:
https://www.youtube.com/watch?v=xrSmf3ipArY

PART 1:
GENERAL INFORMATION

In your own words, define this career.

_____
_____
_____
_____

Job Duties:

_____
_____
_____
_____
_____
_____
_____

Work Environment:

Tools Used:

PART 2:
DETAILED INFORMATION

Education Needed:

_____
_____
_____
_____
_____
_____
_____
_____
_____
_____

Special Skills:

_____
_____
_____
_____
_____
_____
_____
_____
_____
_____
_____

Career Progression:

Part 2:
Detailed Information

Future Outlook:

Other Facts about this Career

PART 3:
PERSONAL ASSESSMENT

Positive Aspects:

_____
_____
_____
_____

Negative Aspects:

_____
_____
_____
_____

Is this Career for you? Why/why not?

A <u>writer</u> produces literary compositions, articles, reports, books, scripts and other texts.

Suggested Websites and Videos:

Gambling and Sports Book Writers and Runners:

https://www.careeronestop.org/toolkit/careers/occupations/occupation-profile.aspx?keyword=Gaming%20and%20Sports%20Book%20Writers%20and%20Runners&onetcode=39301200&location=Maine

Writers and Authors:

https://www.bls.gov/ooh/media-and-communication/writers-and-authors.htm#tab-1

Writers and Authors:

https://www.careeronestop.org/toolkit/careers/occupations/occupation-profile.aspx?keyword=Writers%20and%20Authors&onetcode=27304300&location=georgia&lang=en

Writers and Authors Career Video:

https://www.youtube.com/watch?v=y-5cvUiXW7I

Writers and Authors:

https://www.youtube.com/watch?v=3sNy6kI-8sA

Gaming and Sports Book Writers and Runners:

https://www.youtube.com/watch?v=p6Xis6S-maA

PART 1:
GENERAL INFORMATION

In your own words, define this career.

_____

_____

_____

_____

Job Duties:

_____

_____

_____

_____

_____

_____

_____

Work Environment:

Tools Used:

PART 2:
DETAILED INFORMATION

Education Needed:

_____
_____
_____
_____
_____
_____
_____
_____
_____
_____
_____
_____

Special Skills:

_____
_____
_____
_____
_____
_____
_____
_____
_____
_____
_____

Career Progression:

PART 2: DETAILED INFORMATION

Future Outlook:

Other Facts about this Career

PART 3:
PERSONAL ASSESSMENT

Positive Aspects:

_____
_____
_____
_____

Negative Aspects:

_____
_____
_____
_____

Is this Career for you? Why/why not?

PROGRAMMER

A Programmer

writes and tests code for computer programs and mobile applications.

PROGRAMMER

Suggested Websites and Videos:

Computer Support Specialists:

https://www.bls.gov/ooh/computer-and-information-technology/computer-support-specialists.htm#tab-1

Software Developers, Quality Assurance Analysts, and Testers:

https://www.bls.gov/ooh/computer-and-information-technology/software-developers.htm

Computer Programmers:

https://www.bls.gov/ooh/computer-and-information-technology/computer-programmers.htm

Computer User and Network Support Specialists Career Video:

https://www.youtube.com/watch?v=xe6GS8kSN1g&t=2s

Software Developers Career Video:

https://www.youtube.com/watch?v=_WQ_VV4pXPc

Computer Programmers Career Video:

https://www.youtube.com/watch?v=4FT15GxJQrE

PART 1:
GENERAL INFORMATION

In your own words, define this career.

_____
_____
_____
_____

Job Duties:

_____
_____
_____
_____
_____
_____
_____
_____

Work Environment:

Tools Used:

PART 2:
DETAILED INFORMATION

Education Needed:

_____
_____
_____
_____
_____
_____
_____
_____
_____
_____
_____

Special Skills:

_____
_____
_____
_____
_____
_____
_____
_____
_____
_____
_____
_____

Career Progression:

PART 2:
DETAILED INFORMATION

Future Outlook:

Other Facts about this Career

PART 3:
PERSONAL ASSESSMENT

Positive Aspects:

_____
_____
_____
_____

Negative Aspects:

_____
_____
_____
_____

Is this Career for you? Why/why not?

A Bookkeeper

helps businesses and other organizations keep their finances in order.

Suggested Websites and Videos:

Bookkeeping, Accounting, and Auditing Clerks:
https://www.bls.gov/ooh/office-and-administrative-support/bookkeeping-accounting-and-auditing-clerks.htm

Bookkeeping, Accounting, and Auditing Clerks:
https://www.careeronestop.org/toolkit/careers/occupations/Occupation-profile.aspx?keyword=Bookkeeping,%20Accounting,%20and%20Auditing%20Clerks&onetcode=43303100&ES=Y&EST=accounting+assistant

Bookkeeping, Accounting, and Auditing Clerks:
https://www.onetonline.org/link/summary/43-3031.00

Bookkeeping, Accounting, and Auditing Clerk Career Video:
https://www.youtube.com/watch?v=EsOkxSjUEI0

Bookkeeping Career Overview:
https://www.youtube.com/watch?v=pk8R29u_zu0

Bookkeeping And Accounting - Career Connections - WNEO:
https://www.youtube.com/watch?v=UBX7fPfSIh8

PART 1:
GENERAL INFORMATION

In your own words, define this career.

_____
_____
_____
_____

Job Duties:

_____
_____
_____
_____
_____
_____
_____
_____

Work Environment:

Tools Used:

PART 2:
DETAILED INFORMATION

Education Needed:

_____
_____
_____
_____
_____
_____
_____
_____
_____
_____
_____

Special Skills:

_____
_____
_____
_____
_____
_____
_____
_____
_____
_____
_____
_____

Career Progression:

PART 2:
DETAILED INFORMATION

Future Outlook:

Other Facts about this Career

_____
_____
_____
_____
_____
_____
_____
_____
_____

PART 3:
PERSONAL ASSESSMENT

Positive Aspects:

_____
_____
_____
_____

Negative Aspects:

_____
_____
_____
_____

Is this Career for you? Why/why not?

A Graphic <u>Artist</u> creates artwork that will be used in projects such as advertisements, websites, or book jackets.

Suggested Websites and Videos:

Graphic Designers:

https://www.careeronestop.org/toolkit/careers/occupations/occupation-profile.aspx?keyword=Graphic%20Designers&onetcode=27102400&location=Texas&lang=en

Graphic Designers:

https://www.bls.gov/ooh/arts-and-design/graphic-designers.htm

Graphic Designers:

https://www.onetonline.org/link/summary/27-1024.00

Graphic Designer Career Video:

https://www.youtube.com/watch?v=dt6td67yF9E&t=3s

Graphic Designer - Career Videos:

https://www.youtube.com/watch?v=Ej1ktgOs0lQ

Day at Work: Graphic Designer:

https://www.youtube.com/watch?v=BmBK0_vbYnY

PART 1:
GENERAL INFORMATION

In your own words, define this career.

_____
_____
_____
_____

Job Duties:

_____
_____
_____
_____
_____
_____
_____

Work Environment:

Tools Used:

Part 2:
Detailed Information

Education Needed:

_____
_____
_____
_____
_____
_____
_____
_____
_____
_____
_____
_____

Special Skills:

_____
_____
_____
_____
_____
_____
_____
_____
_____
_____
_____
_____

Career Progression:

PART 2:
DETAILED INFORMATION

Future Outlook:

Other Facts about this Career

_____
_____
_____
_____
_____
_____
_____
_____
_____

PART 3:
PERSONAL ASSESSMENT

Positive Aspects:

_____

_____

_____

_____

Negative Aspects:

_____

_____

_____

_____

Is this Career for you? Why/why not?

A Blogger

produces content and articles for blog posts.

BLOGGER

Suggested Websites and Videos:

Bloggers and webcomic artists: Careers in online creativity:
https://www.bls.gov/careeroutlook/2012/fall/art02.pdf

Social media specialist:
https://www.bls.gov/careeroutlook/2016/youre-a-what/social-media-specialist.htm

Blogger Job Description, Career as a Blogger, Salary, Employment - Definition and Nature of the Work, Education and Training Requirements, Getting the Job -StateUniversity.com:
https://careers.stateuniversity.com/pages/7709/Blogger.html#ixzz 7MIMOPQvE

PART 1:
GENERAL INFORMATION

In your own words, define this career.

_____
_____
_____
_____

Job Duties:

_____
_____
_____
_____
_____
_____
_____

Work Environment:

Tools Used:

PART 2:
DETAILED INFORMATION

Education Needed:

_____
_____
_____
_____
_____
_____
_____
_____
_____
_____
_____
_____

Special Skills:

_____
_____
_____
_____
_____
_____
_____
_____
_____
_____
_____
_____

Career Progression:

PART 2:
DETAILED INFORMATION

Future Outlook:

Other Facts about this Career

_____
_____
_____
_____
_____
_____
_____
_____
_____

PART 3:
PERSONAL ASSESSMENT

Positive Aspects:

_____

_____

_____

_____

Negative Aspects:

_____

_____

_____

_____

Is this Career for you? Why/why not?

A Forest Ranger

preserves and protects our state and national forests, and helps with preventing and fighting fires.

Suggested Websites and Videos:

Forest and Conservation Workers:

https://www.bls.gov/ooh/farming-fishing-and-forestry/forest-and-conservation-workers.htm

Forest and Conservation Workers:

https://www.careeronestop.org/toolkit/careers/occupations/occupation-profile.aspx?keyword=Forest%20and%20Conservation%20Workers&onetcode=45401100&location=US&lang=en

Conservation Officer (Episode 84):

https://www.youtube.com/watch?v=JdxOcGs7MBw

Conservation Scientists Career Video:

https://www.youtube.com/watch?v=PCAudFo7Eo4

Forest and Conservation Worker Career Video:

https://www.youtube.com/watch?v=sOxOWnpaSAQ

Part 1:
General Information

In your own words, define this career.

_____
_____
_____
_____

Job Duties:

_____
_____
_____
_____
_____
_____
_____

Work Environment:

Tools Used:

PART 2:
DETAILED INFORMATION

Education Needed:

_____
_____
_____
_____
_____
_____
_____
_____
_____
_____
_____
_____

Special Skills:

_____
_____
_____
_____
_____
_____
_____
_____
_____
_____
_____

Career Progression:

PART 2:
DETAILED INFORMATION

Future Outlook:

Other Facts about this Career

PART 3:
PERSONAL ASSESSMENT

Positive Aspects:

_____
_____
_____
_____

Negative Aspects:

_____
_____
_____
_____

Is this Career for you? Why/why not?

FARMER

A <u>Farmer</u> grows food and fiber crops for human use.

FARMER

Suggested Websites and Videos:

Farmers, Ranchers, and Other Agricultural Managers:
https://www.bls.gov/ooh/management/farmers-ranchers-and-other-agricultural-managers.htm

Farmers, Ranchers, and Other Agricultural Managers:
https://www.careeronestop.org/toolkit/careers/occupations/occupation-profile.aspx?keyword=Farmers,%20Ranchers,%20and%20Other%20Agricultural%20Managers&onetcode=11901300&location=Alabama

Farmers, Ranchers, and Other Agricultural Managers:
https://www.onetonline.org/link/summary/11-9013.00

11-9013.00 - Farmers, Ranchers, and Other Agricultural Managers:
https://www.youtube.com/watch?v=YoAC6QI_Fx4

Agriculture, Food, and Natural Resources Careers | Career Cluster/Industry Video Series:
https://www.youtube.com/watch?v=erkOXKN9_dQ

Agriculture, Food, and Natural Resources Overview | Career Cluster/Industry Video Series
https://www.youtube.com/watch?v=URaJ4iRu6-o

PART 1:
GENERAL INFORMATION

In your own words, define this career.

_____
_____
_____
_____

Job Duties:

_____
_____
_____
_____
_____
_____
_____

Work Environment:

Tools Used:

PART 2:
DETAILED INFORMATION

Education Needed:

_____
_____
_____
_____
_____
_____
_____
_____
_____
_____
_____
_____

Special Skills:

_____
_____
_____
_____
_____
_____
_____
_____
_____
_____
_____
_____

Career Progression:

PART 2:
DETAILED INFORMATION

Future Outlook:

Other Facts about this Career

_____
_____
_____
_____
_____
_____
_____
_____
_____
_____

PART 3:
PERSONAL ASSESSMENT

Positive Aspects:

_____
_____
_____
_____

Negative Aspects:

_____
_____
_____
_____

Is this Career for you? Why/why not?

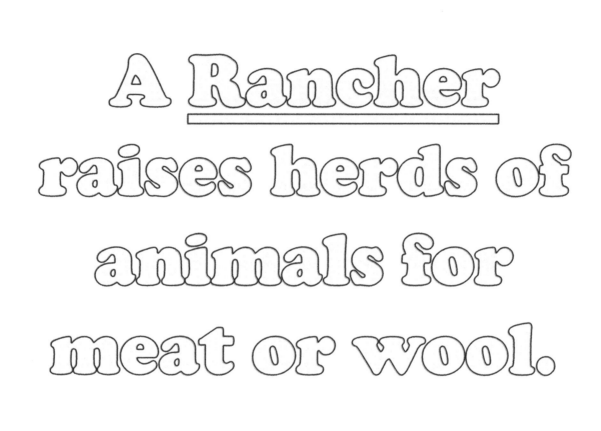

A Rancher

raises herds of animals for meat or wool.

RANCHER

Suggested Websites and Videos:

Farmers, Ranchers, and Other Agricultural Managers:
https://www.bls.gov/ooh/management/farmers-ranchers-and-other-agricultural-managers.htm

Farmers, Ranchers, and Other Agricultural Managers:
https://www.careeronestop.org/toolkit/careers/occupations/occupation-profile.aspx?keyword=Farmers,%20Ranchers,%20and%20Other%20Agricultural%20Managers&onetcode=11901300&location=Alabama

Farmers, Ranchers, and Other Agricultural Managers:
https://www.onetonline.org/link/summary/11-9013.00

11-9013.00 - Farmers, Ranchers, and Other Agricultural Managers:
https://www.youtube.com/watch?v=YoAC6Ql_Fx4

Agriculture, Food, and Natural Resources Careers | Career Cluster/Industry Video Series:
https://www.youtube.com/watch?v=erkOXKN9_dQ

Agriculture, Food, and Natural Resources Overview | Career Cluster/Industry Video Series
https://www.youtube.com/watch?v=URaJ4iRu6-o

PART 1:
GENERAL INFORMATION

In your own words, define this career.

_____
_____
_____
_____

Job Duties:

_____
_____
_____
_____
_____
_____
_____

Work Environment:

Tools Used:

PART 2:
DETAILED INFORMATION

Education Needed:

_____
_____
_____
_____
_____
_____
_____
_____
_____
_____
_____

Special Skills:

_____
_____
_____
_____
_____
_____
_____
_____
_____
_____
_____

Career Progression:

PART 2:
DETAILED INFORMATION

Future Outlook:

Other Facts about this Career

_____
_____
_____
_____
_____
_____
_____
_____
_____

PART 3:
PERSONAL ASSESSMENT

Positive Aspects:

_____

_____

_____

_____

Negative Aspects:

_____

_____

_____

_____

Is this Career for you? Why/why not?

FISHERMAN

A <u>Fisherman</u>
catches or traps fish and marine life to be sold for food or used as bait.

FISHERMAN

Suggested Websites and Videos:

Fishing and Hunting Workers:
https://www.bls.gov/ooh/farming-fishing-and-forestry/fishers-and-related-fishing-workers.htm

Fishing and Hunting Workers:
https://www.careeronestop.org/Toolkit/Careers/Occupations/occupation-profile.aspx?keyword=Fishing%20and%20Hunting%20Workers&onetcode=45303100&location=UNITED%20STATES

Fishing and Hunting Workers:
https://www.onetonline.org/link/summary/45-3031.00

Fishers and Related Fishing Workers Career Video:
https://www.youtube.com/watch?v=zDaL9lJVxow

A Career in Fishing:
https://youtu.be/dxYXwJJKwXM

Manley Jobs: Fishing Guide: EP1:
https://www.youtube.com/watch?v=d1AeIfg4qrA

Part 1:
General Information

In your own words, define this career.

_____

_____

_____

_____

Job Duties:

_____

_____

_____

_____

_____

_____

_____

_____

Work Environment:

Tools Used:

PART 2:
DETAILED INFORMATION

Education Needed:

_____
_____
_____
_____
_____
_____
_____
_____
_____
_____
_____

Special Skills:

_____
_____
_____
_____
_____
_____
_____
_____
_____
_____
_____

Career Progression:

PART 2:
DETAILED INFORMATION

Future Outlook:

Other Facts about this Career

_____
_____
_____
_____
_____
_____
_____
_____
_____
_____

PART 3:
PERSONAL ASSESSMENT

Positive Aspects:

_____
_____
_____
_____

Negative Aspects:

_____
_____
_____
_____

Is this Career for you? Why/why not?

GARDENER

A <u>Gardener</u> plants and maintains landscapes including flowers, bushes, trees, and shrubs.

GARDENER

Suggested Websites and Videos:

Landscaping and Groundskeeping Workers:

https://www.careeronestop.org/Toolkit/Careers/Occupations/occupation-profile.aspx?keyword=Landscaping%20and%20Groundskeeping%20Workers&onetcode=37301100&location=UNITED%20STATES

Farmworkers and Laborers, Crop, Nursery, and Greenhouse:

https://www.careeronestop.org/toolkit/careers/occupations/occupation-profile.aspx?keyword=Farmworkers%20and%20Laborers,%20Crop,%20Nursery,%20and%20Greenhouse&onetcode=45209200&location=Georgia

Grounds Maintenance Workers:

https://www.bls.gov/ooh/building-and-grounds-cleaning/grounds-maintenance-workers.htm

Grounds Maintenance Workers Career Video:

https://www.youtube.com/watch?v=iggxNwURWLY

Grounds Maintenance Worker (Episode 29):

https://www.youtube.com/watch?v=Z_ifQaliaUk

Landscape and Groundskeeping Workers:

https://www.youtube.com/watch?v=7dC4dIRV_Ls

PART 1:
GENERAL INFORMATION

In your own words, define this career.

_____
_____
_____
_____

Job Duties:

_____
_____
_____
_____
_____
_____
_____
_____

Work Environment:

Tools Used:

PART 2:
DETAILED INFORMATION

Education Needed:

_____
_____
_____
_____
_____
_____
_____
_____
_____
_____

Special Skills:

_____
_____
_____
_____
_____
_____
_____
_____
_____
_____
_____
_____

Career Progression:

PART 2:
DETAILED INFORMATION

Future Outlook:

Other Facts about this Career

_____
_____
_____
_____
_____
_____
_____
_____
_____

PART 3:
PERSONAL ASSESSMENT

Positive Aspects:

_____

_____

_____

_____

Negative Aspects:

_____

_____

_____

_____

Is this Career for you? Why/why not?

A Performer

entertains audiences through dance, music, acting or other creative endeavor.

PERFORMER

Suggested Websites and Videos:

What does a Performer Do?
https://www.careerexplorer.com/careers/performer/

Performing Arts Career Info and Resources
https://www.thebalancecareers.com/performing-arts-jobs-525936

Musicians and Singers
https://www.bls.gov/ooh/entertainment-and-sports/musicians-and-singers.htm

Dancers and Choreographers
https://collegegrad.com/careers/dancers-and-choreographers

How to Build a Career as a Performer
https://www.youtube.com/watch?v=SMxnSdArIGc

Career Paths and a Social Awareness for the Dancer: Commercial Performer
https://www.youtube.com/watch?v=95xOpcmxJx4

Broadway Dancer Explains Her Career Path, from First Job to Current | Teen Vogue
https://www.youtube.com/watch?v=VvGum3OEmtk

Careers For Musicians - Exploring Musician Jobs with a Pro
https://www.youtube.com/watch?v=QaxzW1RtnyY

Part 1:
General Information

In your own words, define this career.

_____
_____
_____
_____

Job Duties:

_____
_____
_____
_____
_____
_____
_____

Work Environment:

Tools Used:

PART 2:
DETAILED INFORMATION

Education Needed:

_____
_____
_____
_____
_____
_____
_____
_____
_____
_____
_____

Special Skills:

_____
_____
_____
_____
_____
_____
_____
_____
_____
_____
_____

Career Progression:

PART 2:
DETAILED INFORMATION

Future Outlook:

Other Facts about this Career

_____
_____
_____
_____
_____
_____
_____
_____
_____
_____

PART 3:
PERSONAL ASSESSMENT

Positive Aspects:

_____
_____
_____
_____

Negative Aspects:

_____
_____
_____
_____

Is this Career for you? Why/why not?

A Painter can either apply paint, stain, and coatings to walls and other structures or create works of art on various surfaces.

Suggested Websites and Videos:

Craft and Fine Artists:
>   https://www.bls.gov/ooh/arts-and-design/craft-and-fine-artists.htm

How to become a Painter
>   https://www.indeed.com/career/painter/career-advice

How to Become a Painter
>   https://www.becomeopedia.com/painter/

So You Want to be a Commercial Painter
>   https://www.youtube.com/watch?v=Zlo8nPh38Lk

TURNING ART INTO A CAREER- How I make $250K/ Year
>   https://www.youtube.com/watch?v=gvvUmb3b2eo

Getting started as an ARTIST - my 5 Top Tips!
>   https://www.youtube.com/watch?v=bhpnb7r9Vw0

Craft Artist Career Video:
>   https://www.youtube.com/watch?v=T_X9ZdUq-2Q

PART 1:
GENERAL INFORMATION

In your own words, define this career.

_____
_____
_____
_____

Job Duties:

_____
_____
_____
_____
_____
_____
_____
_____

Work Environment:

Tools Used:

PART 2:
DETAILED INFORMATION

Education Needed:

_____
_____
_____
_____
_____
_____
_____
_____
_____
_____
_____

Special Skills:

_____
_____
_____
_____
_____
_____
_____
_____
_____
_____
_____

Career Progression:

PART 2:
DETAILED INFORMATION

Future Outlook:

Other Facts about this Career

_____
_____
_____
_____
_____
_____
_____
_____
_____
_____

PART 3:
PERSONAL ASSESSMENT

Positive Aspects:

_____

_____

_____

_____

Negative Aspects:

_____

_____

_____

_____

Is this Career for you? Why/why not?

An Inventor

creates or discovers an invention that meets a need.

 Suggested Websites and Videos:

Inventor:

https://www.okcollegestart.org/Career_Planning/Career_Profile/Career_Profile.aspx?id=2fXAP2FPAXjhVySW2MR2dXAP2FPAXEGshnAwXAP3DPAXXAP3DPAX

How to Become an Inventor

https://www.indeed.com/career-advice/finding-a-job/how-to-become-inventor

Web and Digital Interface Designers:

https://www.onetonline.org/link/summary/15-1255.00

How to become an Inventor

https://moviecultists.com/how-to-become-an-inventor

How to Invent Something New in Five Easy Steps and Become an Inventor

https://www.youtube.com/watch?v=ZiF-ZuW3-BI

PART 1:
GENERAL INFORMATION

In your own words, define this career.

_____
_____
_____
_____

Job Duties:

_____
_____
_____
_____
_____
_____

Work Environment:

Tools Used:

PART 2:
DETAILED INFORMATION

Education Needed:

_____
_____
_____
_____
_____
_____
_____
_____
_____
_____
_____

Special Skills:

_____
_____
_____
_____
_____
_____
_____
_____
_____
_____
_____

Career Progression:

PART 2:
DETAILED INFORMATION

Future Outlook:

Other Facts about this Career

_____
_____
_____
_____
_____
_____
_____
_____
_____

PART 3:
PERSONAL ASSESSMENT

Positive Aspects:

_____

_____

_____

_____

Negative Aspects:

_____

_____

_____

_____

Is this Career for you? Why/why not?

A Chef prepares food and oversees the kitchens in restaurants and other establishments.

Suggested Websites and Videos:

Chefs and Head Cooks:

https://www.bls.gov/ooh/food-preparation-and-serving/chefs-and-head-cooks.htm

Chefs and Head Cooks:

https://www.careeronestop.org/toolkit/careers/occupations/occupation-profile.aspx?keyword=Chefs%20and%20Head%20Cooks&onetcode=35101100&location=Massachusetts&onet=35101100

Chefs and Head Cooks:

https://www.onetonline.org/link/summary/35-1011.00

Chefs and Head Cooks Career Video:

https://www.youtube.com/watch?v=BtAevVMysC0

Executive Chef Irv, Career Video from drkit.org:

https://www.youtube.com/watch?v=4Qf3BERapEA

Chef Career Overview:

https://www.youtube.com/watch?v=usEmBNoBuG0

PART 1:
GENERAL INFORMATION

In your own words, define this career.

_____
_____
_____
_____

Job Duties:

_____
_____
_____
_____
_____
_____
_____
_____

Work Environment:

Tools Used:

PART 2:
DETAILED INFORMATION

Education Needed:

_____
_____
_____
_____
_____
_____
_____
_____
_____
_____
_____
_____

Special Skills:

_____
_____
_____
_____
_____
_____
_____
_____
_____
_____
_____
_____

Career Progression:

PART 2:
DETAILED INFORMATION

Future Outlook:

Other Facts about this Career

_____
_____
_____
_____
_____
_____
_____
_____
_____
_____

PART 3:
PERSONAL ASSESSMENT

Positive Aspects:

_____

_____

_____

_____

Negative Aspects:

_____

_____

_____

_____

Is this Career for you? Why/why not?

BEAUTICIAN

A Beautician

provides cosmetology services such as hair, nail, makeup or skin care.

BEAUTICIAN

Suggested Websites and Videos:

Barbers, Hairstylists, and Cosmetologists:
https://www.bls.gov/ooh/personal-care-and-service/barbers-hairstylists-and-cosmetologists.htm

Barbers, Hairstylists, and Cosmetologists:
https://www.careeronestop.org/Toolkit/Careers/Occupations/occupation-profile.aspx?keyword=Hairdressers,%20Hairstylists,%20and%20Cosmetologists&location=UNITED%20STATES&onetcode=39501200

Hairstylists, and Cosmetologists:
https://www.onetonline.org/link/summary/39-5012.00

Barbers:
https://www.onetonline.org/link/summary/39-5011.00

Hairdressers, Hairstylists, Barbers, and Cosmetologists Career Video:
https://www.youtube.com/watch?v=wqgol3sEFvI

Hair Stylist, Career Video from drkit.org:
https://www.youtube.com/watch?v=z07baQZyNlg

Hairstylist, Career Video from drkit.org:
https://www.youtube.com/watch?v=SIvLILoM4ZM

PART 1:
GENERAL INFORMATION

In your own words, define this career.

_____
_____
_____
_____

Job Duties:

_____
_____
_____
_____
_____
_____
_____
_____

Work Environment:

Tools Used:

PART 2:
DETAILED INFORMATION

Education Needed:

_____
_____
_____
_____
_____
_____
_____
_____
_____
_____
_____

Special Skills:

_____
_____
_____
_____
_____
_____
_____
_____
_____
_____
_____
_____

Career Progression:

PART 2:
DETAILED INFORMATION

Future Outlook:

Other Facts about this Career

_____
_____
_____
_____
_____
_____
_____
_____
_____

PART 3:
PERSONAL ASSESSMENT

Positive Aspects:

_____

_____

_____

_____

Negative Aspects:

_____

_____

_____

_____

Is this Career for you? Why/why not?

A <u>Groomer</u> is responsible for improving an animal's hygiene and appearance.

GROOMER

Suggested Websites and Videos:

Animal Care and Service Workers:
https://www.bls.gov/ooh/personal-care-and-service/animal-care-and-service-workers.htm

Animal Caretakers:
https://www.careeronestop.org/Toolkit/Careers/Occupations/occupation-profile.aspx?keyword=Nonfarm%20Animal%20Caretakers&location=UNITED%20STATES&onetcode=39202100

Animal Caretakers:
https://www.onetonline.org/link/summary/39-2021.00

Nonfarm Animal Caretaker Career Video:
https://www.youtube.com/watch?v=REIGWH6Tedw&t=1s

Veterinary Assistants and Laboratory Animal Caretakers Career Video:
https://www.youtube.com/watch?v=M7H9heVK-I4

Animal Care Specialist, Career Video from drkit.org:
https://www.youtube.com/watch?v=yCUqBYvfeJ0

PART 1:
GENERAL INFORMATION

In your own words, define this career.

_____

_____

_____

_____

Job Duties:

_____

_____

_____

_____

_____

_____

_____

Work Environment:

Tools Used:

PART 2:
DETAILED INFORMATION

Education Needed:

_____
_____
_____
_____
_____
_____
_____
_____
_____
_____

Special Skills:

_____
_____
_____
_____
_____
_____
_____
_____
_____
_____

Career Progression:

PART 2:
DETAILED INFORMATION

Future Outlook:

Other Facts about this Career

_____
_____
_____
_____
_____
_____
_____
_____
_____
_____

PART 3:
PERSONAL ASSESSMENT

Positive Aspects:

_____
_____
_____
_____

Negative Aspects:

_____
_____
_____
_____

Is this Career for you? Why/why not?

A Travel Agent

helps people plan destinations and trip itineraries, and makes travel arrangements.

Travel Agent

Suggested Websites and Videos:

Travel Agents:
https://www.bls.gov/ooh/sales/travel-agents.htm

Travel Agents:
https://www.careeronestop.org/Toolkit/Careers/Occupations/occupation-profile.aspx?keyword=Travel%20Agents&location=UNITED%20STATES&onetcode=41304100

Travel Agents:
https://www.onetonline.org/link/summary/41-3041.00

Travel Agents Career Video:
https://www.youtube.com/watch?v=2GEPp0P4Yto

Travel Agent - Career Video:
https://www.youtube.com/watch?v=IzvK_WzM8cQ

Travel Agent Careers Overview:
https://www.youtube.com/watch?v=HNJBMSPoYiE

Part 1:
General Information

In your own words, define this career.

_____
_____
_____
_____

Job Duties:

_____
_____
_____
_____
_____
_____
_____

Work Environment:

Tools Used:

PART 2:
DETAILED INFORMATION

Education Needed:

_____
_____
_____
_____
_____
_____
_____
_____
_____
_____
_____
_____

Special Skills:

_____
_____
_____
_____
_____
_____
_____
_____
_____
_____
_____
_____

Career Progression:

PART 2:
DETAILED INFORMATION

Future Outlook:

Other Facts about this Career

PART 3:
PERSONAL ASSESSMENT

Positive Aspects:

_____
_____
_____
_____

Negative Aspects:

_____
_____
_____
_____

Is this Career for you? Why/why not?

A <u>Realtor</u> helps people buy and sell real estate.

Suggested Websites and Videos:

Real Estate Brokers and Sales Agents:

https://www.bls.gov/ooh/sales/real-estate-brokers-and-sales-agents.htm

Real Estate Sales Agents:

https://www.careeronestop.org/toolkit/careers/occupations/occupation-profile.aspx?keyword=Real%20Estate%20Sales%20Agents&onetcode=41902200&location=UNITED%20STATES&onet=41902200

Real Estate Brokers:

https://www.careeronestop.org/toolkit/careers/occupations/Occupation-profile.aspx?keyword=Real%20Estate%20Brokers&onetcode=41902100&location=US

Real Estate Agents and Brokers Career Video:

https://www.youtube.com/watch?v=Fh03puSzv7g

Real Estate Broker, Career Video from drkit.org:

https://www.youtube.com/watch?v=xqDMgjd5_K8

Real Estate Agent - Career Video:

https://www.youtube.com/watch?v=JgwRonqtdwY

PART 1:
GENERAL INFORMATION

In your own words, define this career.

_____
_____
_____
_____

Job Duties:

_____
_____
_____
_____
_____
_____
_____
_____

Work Environment:

Tools Used:

PART 2:
DETAILED INFORMATION

Education Needed:

_____
_____
_____
_____
_____
_____
_____
_____
_____
_____
_____
_____

Special Skills:

_____
_____
_____
_____
_____
_____
_____
_____
_____
_____
_____
_____

Career Progression:

PART 2:
DETAILED INFORMATION

Future Outlook:

Other Facts about this Career

_____
_____
_____
_____
_____
_____
_____
_____
_____

PART 3:
PERSONAL ASSESSMENT

Positive Aspects:

_____
_____
_____
_____

Negative Aspects:

_____
_____
_____
_____

Is this Career for you? Why/why not?

A Nanny partners with parents to help raise and provide care for children.

Suggested Websites and Videos:

Childcare Workers:

https://www.bls.gov/ooh/personal-care-and-service/childcare-workers.htm

Nannies:

https://www.careeronestop.org/toolkit/careers/occupations/occupation-profile.aspx?keyword=Nannies&onetcode=39901101&location=UNITED%20STATES&lang=en

Nannies:

https://www.onetonline.org/link/summary/39-9011.01

Childcare Workers Career Video:

https://www.youtube.com/watch?v=xjYk0w_MMmw&t=1s

Childcare Workers Nanny Career Information :

https://www.youtube.com/watch?v=L80wih8K9BM

Nanny Job Description:

https://www.youtube.com/watch?v=y8DOSTim6fM

Part 1:
General Information

In your own words, define this career.

_____
_____
_____
_____

Job Duties:

_____
_____
_____
_____
_____
_____
_____

Work Environment:

Tools Used:

PART 2:
DETAILED INFORMATION

Education Needed:

_____
_____
_____
_____
_____
_____
_____
_____
_____
_____
_____

Special Skills:

_____
_____
_____
_____
_____
_____
_____
_____
_____
_____
_____

Career Progression:

PART 2:
DETAILED INFORMATION

Future Outlook:

Other Facts about this Career

_____
_____
_____
_____
_____
_____
_____
_____
_____
_____

PART 3:
PERSONAL ASSESSMENT

Positive Aspects:

_____

_____

_____

_____

Negative Aspects:

_____

_____

_____

_____

Is this Career for you? Why/why not?

Free Choice Careers

Have a career idea of your own you want to explore?

Throughout this course you have been exposed to many different career choices. But perhaps the one you are interested in exploring wasn't in here. Or perhaps you just want to continue your spotlight explorations past the limitations of this course.

In this section you will find three free choice career exploration groups of pages. This is your opportunity to explore careers beyond those that you have experienced so far. We have included a blank website and video page for you to record the sources that you use during your explorations. Then just fill out the exploration pages as you did with the other careers in this course.

So keep going. Seek. Discover. Explore.

Career Worth Exploring:

Design a decorative definition or explanation of your career.

Career Exploration:

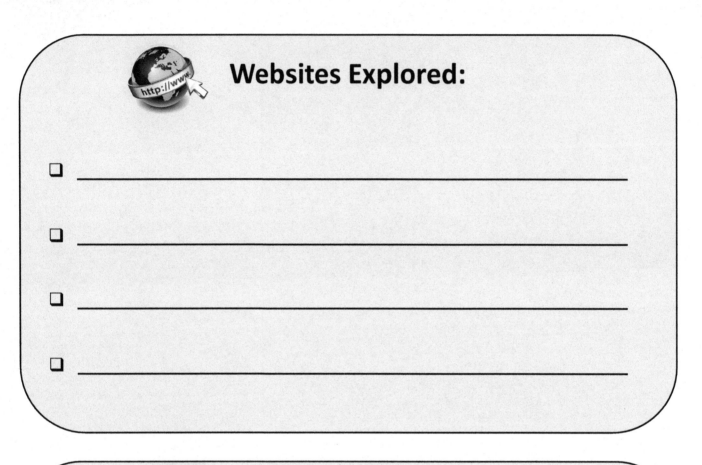

Websites Explored:

- ☐ _____
- ☐ _____
- ☐ _____
- ☐ _____

Videos Watched:

- ☐ _____
- ☐ _____
- ☐ _____
- ☐ _____

PART 1:
GENERAL INFORMATION

In your own words, define this career.

_____
_____
_____
_____

Job Duties:

_____
_____
_____
_____
_____
_____

Work Environment:

Tools Used:

PART 2:
DETAILED INFORMATION

Education Needed:

_____
_____
_____
_____
_____
_____
_____
_____
_____
_____
_____

Special Skills:

_____
_____
_____
_____
_____
_____
_____
_____
_____
_____
_____
_____

Career Progression:

Part 2:
Detailed Information

Future Outlook:

Other Facts about this Career

PART 3:
PERSONAL ASSESSMENT

Positive Aspects:

_____
_____
_____
_____

Negative Aspects:

_____
_____
_____
_____

Is this Career for you? Why/why not?

Career Worth Exploring:

Career Worth Exploring:

Design a decorative definition or explanation of your career.

CAREER EXPLORATION:

Websites Explored:

- ☐ _____
- ☐ _____
- ☐ _____
- ☐ _____

Videos Watched:

- ☐ _____
- ☐ _____
- ☐ _____
- ☐ _____

PART 1:
GENERAL INFORMATION

In your own words, define this career.

_____
_____
_____
_____

Job Duties:

_____
_____
_____
_____
_____
_____
_____

Work Environment:

Tools Used:

PART 2:
DETAILED INFORMATION

Education Needed:

_____
_____
_____
_____
_____
_____
_____
_____
_____
_____
_____
_____

Special Skills:

_____
_____
_____
_____
_____
_____
_____
_____
_____
_____
_____
_____

Career Progression:

PART 2:
DETAILED INFORMATION

Future Outlook:

Other Facts about this Career

PART 3:
PERSONAL ASSESSMENT

Positive Aspects:

_____

_____

_____

_____

Negative Aspects:

_____

_____

_____

_____

Is this Career for you? Why/why not?

Career Worth Exploring:

Design a decorative definition or explanation of your career.

Career Exploration:

Websites Explored:

☐ _____

☐ _____

☐ _____

☐ _____

Videos Watched:

☐ _____

☐ _____

☐ _____

☐ _____

Part 1:
General Information

In your own words, define this career.

_____

_____

_____

_____

Job Duties:

_____

_____

_____

_____

_____

_____

_____

Work Environment:

Tools Used:

PART 2:
DETAILED INFORMATION

Education Needed:

_____
_____
_____
_____
_____
_____
_____
_____
_____
_____

Special Skills:

_____
_____
_____
_____
_____
_____
_____
_____
_____
_____

Career Progression:

PART 2:
DETAILED INFORMATION

Future Outlook:

Other Facts about this Career

_____
_____
_____
_____
_____
_____
_____
_____
_____
_____

PART 3:
PERSONAL ASSESSMENT

Positive Aspects:

_____

_____

_____

_____

Negative Aspects:

_____

_____

_____

_____

Is this Career for you? Why/why not?

About
Exploring
Expression

Welcome to Exploring Expression

Brandy Champeau

Nancy Holt

Exploring Expression is a Leader in Cross-Curricular, Project-based curriculum and unit studies for both children and adults.

At Exploring Expression, we focus on 4 specific offerings:

1. We build quality learning resources for K12 students
2. We create resources for parents and educators to help them become the best expressions of themselves and equip them to better facilitate learning opportunities for their children
3. We utilize public speaking platforms to spread the message of becoming the best expression of yourself through the cultivation of a learning lifestyle
4. We help people with a message and a passion for learning find their voice, publish their books and create curriculum or training to share with the world

As you can see, our passion is learning - learning about yourself and learning about the world. We focus on self-improvement and education. Because in the end it all comes down to learning. Learning doesn't have to be hard and it doesn't have to be boring. At Exploring Expression we want to help you put the engagement and excitement back into education and to put the education back into life.

Contact Us!

 https://ExploringExpression.com

 www.facebook.com/ExploringExpression

 www.Instagram.com/ExploringExpression

 www.twitter.com/ExExAdmin

 https://bit.ly/2KZrSFG

Check out these other Books and Courses by Exploring Expression

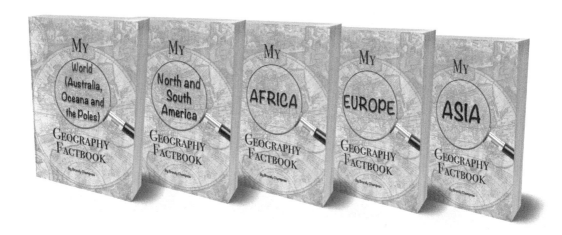

Order these and more at https://ExploringExpression.com

Made in the USA
Columbia, SC
11 February 2023

11470625R10187